The Pre-existence of the Sabbath

By Maurice Caines

TEACH Services, Inc.
PUBLISHING
www.TEACHServices.com • (800) 367-1844

Copyright © 2013 TEACH Services, Inc.
ISBN-13: 978-1-4796-0186-8 (Paperback)
ISBN-13: 978-1-4796-0187-5 (ePub)
ISBN-13: 978-1-4796-0188-2 (Mobi)

All scripture quotations, unless otherwise indicated, are taken from the King James Version. Public domain.

Published by

TEACH Services, Inc.
P U B L I S H I N G
www.TEACHServices.com ● (800) 367-1844

Contents

A Gem of Truth

During a recent study of the Bible, I came across an enlightening discovery in the book of Genesis. Passages of Scripture I had read many times before helped me to discover that the seventh-day Sabbath, established on earth after God ended His work of creation, existed even before the Garden of Eden. I recognized this gem of truth as an important blessing from the treasury of God's holy Word. I prayed for more insights from God and asked for guidance from the Holy Spirit as to how I could share with others what the Lord gave me through divine inspiration.

Scripture teaches that the heavenly angels are engaged in a ceaseless demonstration of worship before God. They acknowledge His divine sovereignty and glory as the great I Am. The angelic proclamation of praise and adoration for the Creator of heaven and earth takes place in an atmosphere that is far superior to any form of worship on earth. Yet it highlights the inherent nature and purpose of the Sabbath, which was made for man.

God sanctified the first Sabbath day after the creation of the earth. In doing this, He gave to humanity the wonderful privilege of cooperating with the angels in His great and harmonious purposes of worship for heaven and earth. So the Sabbath is seen as a symbol of the nature of God.

In giving the Sabbath to man, God clearly demonstrated His desire to allow human beings to develop individual loyalty in choosing to worship the only true and living God. As a memorial of creation, the Sabbath reminds us that we are created beings living in the presence of Omnipotence. This realization should be clearest when we are in a state of worship before Him each Sabbath.

Because of the limitations of our humanity, our worship is flawed by the effect of sin. Yet the memorial of the Sabbath that comes to us on the seventh day of each week gives us the chance to increase our understanding of what takes place in heaven on a continuous basis in the presence of our holy God in that atmosphere of worship.

The truth of that passage that I read in Genesis further revealed to me that God created the Sabbath for the spiritual needs of humanity. As soon as the earth was created, God instituted the Sabbath because people needed this external reminder to maintain their sense of awe and worship towards their Creator. Once Adam and Eve sinned, humanity was in even greater need of this memorial of the creation. Its purpose now is to lead us back to our Creator.

Scripture states that God rested from all his work, and this has been made an example to us in keeping the Sabbath. In this way, we demonstrate our compliance with His divine will. Since God's law is of God's divine nature, and He is eternal, then it follows that the Sabbath is also eternal. So then if the law is eternal as God is, the Sabbath had to have its presence long before our creation and even the angels.

When we contemplate the worship given to God by the angels, we realize that the most significant aspect of the Sabbath is worship. The Sabbath brings us into harmony with God's will, for it embodies the system of worship that existed in heaven before our creation. The twenty-four-hour period of the seventh day that has been established for rest and worship is part of God's plan for this earth. This plan will not be changed when our worship commences in the eternal realms of the new heaven and earth where complete righteousness will dwell forever. There we are told that we will come together to worship before God from one Sabbath to the next (see Isa. 66:23).

So we see that the Sabbath continues because God formulated it based upon His eternal nature. The angels who worship him will continue to do so for eternity. Soon the redeemed of all the ages will join them in continuous worship before God. They will worship Him forever in the earth made new, as a result of their redemption and restoration through the grace of our eternal Savior and Lord, Jesus Christ.

I believe that the word "Sabbath" is a name given to humans, teaching them how to relate to this day of utmost importance. That name for God's holy day is essentially a construct that gives us an idea of what heaven is like in that atmosphere of worship. It always helps humanity to understand something of what it will be like to live in the presence of our holy God at the fulfillment of our redemption.

The moral law is a reflection of God's infinite character. God not only made the Sabbath, and sanctified it for a memorial, but He also engraved it as one of the first four commandments in His holy law. As one of the Ten Commandments, the keeping of the Sabbath is mandatory for all God's creatures.

It has to be true that the heavenly angels keep the commandments of God. We know this because one third of them were judged for breaking the first commandment, which states, "Thou shalt have no other gods before me" (Exod. 20:3). It was by their bad choice that they smeared God's character before all of His other created beings. And in spite of God's loving entreaties, they demonstrated their unwillingness to repent and worship their Creator. Ultimately, they were cast out of heaven for their disobedience to God's law.

There are several more evidences in Scripture that God's law is eternal:

- Throughout the Bible, the eternal God is shown to be holy, just, good, and perfect in righteousness. These same words are used to describe His holy law. "Wherefore the law is holy, and the commandment holy, and just, and good" (Rom. 7:12).

- There is nothing new to God, because He is omniscient. It is this atmosphere of worship on the Sabbath day that makes me believe that the Sabbath must have existed before it was established in Eden after the six days of creation because it is shown to be in that oneness of worship to

God only, as is the angels in heaven, being a part of that perfect law, which demonstrates His unchanging character.

- God's plan for dealing with those angels who were deceived by Lucifer was based upon the eternal nature of His law—His character.
- Similarly, God's plan by which human beings could find their way back to God after the fall of Adam and Eve was based upon the eternal nature of His unchanging law of love.

The path has been cleared to redeem humanity, and to repair the damage done by Lucifer and the fallen angels. We may receive God's gift of salvation as long as we don't persist in rejecting His law as the fallen angels did. One could surmise that we have become spiritual opportunists in this regard for God offers the same plan of redemption to us that was also made for angels. This may be an inference of truth, but let's consider the facts. The first sinner was Lucifer, and the law that he transgressed in heaven is the same law that now governs humanity here on earth, which we also have transgressed. How could there be a plan of salvation and redemption for humanity, who came on the scene of sin afterwards, if there was none for Lucifer who sinned first in heaven itself and violated the same law of God?

When the fallen angels became conceited and chose to support Lucifer, the first sinner in heaven, those angels were also condemned with him. Consequently, when Adam became conceited and chose to follow the first sinner of earth, Eve, he was also condemned with her. God drove Adam and Eve out of their home, the Garden of Eden, similar to His divine act of banishing Lucifer and the fallen angels from their home in heaven. Although both were banished from their respective home because of their sin, there is a vast spiritual difference between Lucifer and Adam. When the consequences of sin were presented, Adam accepted God's plan of salvation and redemption whereas Lucifer did not.

I believe it is safe to infer that there was a period in heaven when some measure of divine counseling took place to help discourage Lucifer in pursuing the path of his rebellion. "God in His great mercy bore long with Lucifer. He was not immediately degraded from his exalted station when he first indulged the spirit of discontent, nor even when he began to present his false claims before the loyal angels. Long was he retained in heaven. Again and again he was offered pardon on condition of repentance and submission. Such efforts as only infinite love and wisdom could devise were made to convince him of his error.... Lucifer was convinced that he was in the wrong, that the divine claims were just, and that he ought to acknowledge them as such before all heaven. Had he done this, he might have saved himself and many angels" (Ellen G. White, *The Great Controversy*, pp. 495, 496).

Adam and Eve, when they met with God in the cool of the day, listened as He laid out the dangers of sin and encouraged them to obey His commandments. Sadly, they disobeyed. Yet, Adam and Eve and their descendants are the creation that are divinely privileged, according to the power of their choices, to be redeemed through the grace and death of our Lord Jesus Christ. So what does choice have to do in all of this? It comes down to a matter of willingness—willingness to obey God's law. This decision rests upon all God's children here on earth and throughout the universe.

To our feeble, earthbound minds, God's immutable and holy law often gives support to His character of love and His gracious invitations of mercy. As the earthly sanctuary models the heavenly sanctuary, it teaches humanity how to deal with its spiritual ministry and worship to God. In the same manner, the Ten Commandments model for earthlings the governing principles of the laws of heaven.

In 1 Corinthians 6:3 Paul writes, "Know ye not that we shall judge angels?" This can only be the case if we are governed by the same rule of law that governs the heavenly beings. In essence, there is only one law and that law is the law of heaven. The law given by God to humans is simply a duplicate of the law that rules the universe. God is all about unity and impartiality. There is only one God, and one law. Obedience to that law is the highest form of worship and a sign of our loyalty. Walking in harmony with the principles of the law leads the soul into adoration and joy in communion with the one true and living God.

In Psalm 8:5 and Hebrews 2:7 we can see that the angels were created a little higher than humans. The adoration and praise with which they worship is beyond our earthly comprehension because they can see and understand God in ways that are still beyond our understanding. Lucifer and his angels rebelled against God's government with their eyes wide open to the full extent of God's goodness and with complete knowledge of the loving perfection of heaven's system of governance. The one-third of the angels who rejected the law of heaven could not remain there because their determined choice to live in sin set them eternally against the principles of goodness that governed them in heaven.

When humans traded God's truth for Lucifer's lies, they entered into the same sins that caused the rebel angels to be removed from heaven. In essence, they traded the government of God for the government of Satan. For this reason, Adam and Eve were then driven from their perfect Eden home.

But there is a difference between the sin of Adam and Eve, and the sin of Lucifer and his angels. Adam and Eve had enough evidence of God's goodness, which they used, unlike the fallen angels, to trust God, yet there was much more for the earthly pair to learn about the differences between God's government and that of their new sovereign, Satan, through the plan of salvation. They did not have the benefit of having observed the full light of heaven's glory first hand. They did not consciously set out to destroy the government of God as did the fallen angels. Eve was beguiled—tricked, but Adam volunteered himself because of his love for Eve became sinful of himself by joining her in sin instead of trusting in God at first, to solve the problem. For this fallen couple there was still hope that a fuller experience with the differences between God's government and that of Satan would lead them to repent of their sin and surrender fully to God. Thus, He has given us the Ten Commandments as a model of heaven's covenant principles applied here on the earth.

We are created beings like the angels. The law of God reminds us to worship Him only. By identifying each day with a numerical name leading up to the seventh-day Sabbath, and by designating the sixth day as "the preparation" (Exod. 16:5; Mark 15:42), He established a daily reminder of the worship, which we owe to Him as our Creator. It is evident that the seventh-day Sabbath existed before the creation of this earth, as we have seen by its infinite placement within the eternal law of God.

Genesis 1:1–31 teaches us that God created the world in six literal days. This creation included everything from the smallest one-celled creatures to human beings. On each of the days of creation, God confirmed each completion by saying that "the evening and the morning" were the first day through the sixth day.

In Genesis 2:1–3 God ceased from His creative work. The seventh day, however, was very different from the previous six days as God did not speak the same words for the seventh day as he did for the previous six days. He did not say "the evening and the morning" were the seventh day. I believe that God omitted those words for a special reason.

Could God have forgotten these words? Of course not! Obviously it was all about a difference in the nature of that seventh day. For on that day, the eternal God was establishing a link between heaven and earth. He was synchronizing the worship of humanity with the worship in heaven. For man, that special time of communion with God was made to be embodied within a twenty-four hour span at the creation of the seventh day. As we can see, God established this seventh day as a time when we can come together to spend time in fellowship with Him as He did with Adam and Eve in an atmosphere of worship.

> Thus the heavens and the earth were finished, and all the host of them. And on the seventh day God ended his work which he had made; and he rested on the seventh day from all his

work which he had made. And God blessed the seventh day, and sanctified it: because that in it he had rested from all his work which God created and made. (Gen. 2:3)

The first six days are specifically said to be made up of "the evening and the morning," yet you will notice that there is no mention of "the evening and morning" with regard to the seventh day. The nature of the Sabbath is clearly different from that of the other six days. The Sabbath, which was "made for man" (Mark 2:27), came from the eternal existence that it already had with God. The Sabbath has an eternal purpose, and humanity is privileged to take part in that eternal purpose, not only for human beings, but for all of God's creation throughout the universe.

The first earthly Sabbath was celebrated first by God, and then Adam and Eve joined Him on that first "seventh day" that marked the birth of this earth. God rested, and ceased from all His creative activities. Of course He did not physically need the rest, for He is the Omnipotent One; but His divine rest served as an example for all humanity. The second divine activity was that of blessing this particular day.

God had already blessed the birds, the fishes, Adam and Eve, and all other created things during the first six days of creation week. On those days we see that a blessing was given to objects and creatures, but not to the day itself. Therefore, God's blessing placed upon the seventh day sets it apart spiritually from the other days. It was designed for a special purpose. The blessing bestowed upon the seventh day by the Creator Himself was intended to make it spiritually beneficial to humanity, beginning with Adam and Eve.

The holy atmosphere of worship on that seventh day is seen as the crowning act of His creative work. This gives us yet another idea of the similarity in what we do at the end of each weekly cycle when we come together with God, giving thanks to Him for the blessings of those six days of labor and work. The seventh day is made for worship.

Even though Adam was given "dominion" over the animals, birds, fishes, and everything else on the entire earth, the Sabbath was a weekly reminder that Adam's dominion was subject to the ultimate sovereignty of the Creator God who made everything in the first place. This reminder of God's sovereignty was to be binding upon all the descendants of Adam and Eve forever. Thus, the Sabbath not only memorialized creation, but it is also the day to worship God as Creator and Ruler of earth and heaven.

This responsibility was again spelled out in detail when the Ten Commandments were given to God's people on Mount Sinai and were clearly outlined in the fourth commandment. There we see that the sons and daughters, the manservants and maidservants, and even the animals within the gates of Sabbath keepers are to rest on the seventh day. Animals may not be capable of observing the Sabbath, yet because of the dominion of humanity over them, he was charged to allow them the benefits of the Sabbath rest as outlined in the fourth Commandment (see Exod. 20:10).

Notice that God sanctified the seventh day. He set it apart for a holy use. God gave this special Sabbath day to the first members of the human race, making it evident that the Sabbath is intended for all of their descendants. The fourth commandment (Exod. 20:8) requires humanity to "remember" that God established the seventh-day Sabbath at the creation of the world.

Therefore, it is inspiration like the following quote that establishes the facts that the Bible still holds many more gems of spiritual treasures that will be unfolded in these last days to re-enforce the truth that is already divinely established through God's Word. In *The Great Controversy* Ellen White writes: "And still there will arise, new heights to surmount; new wonders to admire; new truths to comprehend; fresh objects to call forth the powers of the mind, soul and body" (p. 677).

Take a moment to read 1 Corinthians 2:10–14:

> But God hath revealed them unto us by his Spirit: for the Spirit searcheth all things, yea, the deep things of God. For what man knoweth the things of a man, save the spirit of man which is in him? even so the things of God knoweth no man, but the Spirit of God. Now we have received, not the spirit of the world, but the spirit which is of God; that we might know the things that are freely given to us of God. Which things also we speak, not in the words which man's wisdom teacheth, but which the Holy Ghost teacheth; comparing spiritual things with spiritual. But the natural man receiveth not the things of the Spirit of God: for they are foolishness unto

> him: neither can he know them, be-
> cause they are spiritually discerned.

It is my belief that the study of these things in the light of God's Word will give more divine validation to the eternal and everlasting existence of God's holy day, the seventh day Sabbath of rest, here on earth. Please note that this seventh-day Sabbath is the only day distinguished by an eternal existence, and its purpose is different from the other Sabbath days mentioned in the Bible. The seventh-day Sabbath is the only Sabbath written by the finger of God in His law.

The ceremonial Sabbaths had a temporary purpose and were mainly used as "the shadow of things to come" (see 2 Chron. 8:13; Neh. 10:33; Isa. 1:13). This is made plain in Colossians 2:14, 16, 17, which reads:

> Blotting out the handwriting of ordinances that was against us, which was contrary to us, and took it out of the way, nailing it to his cross … Let no man therefore judge you in meat, or in drink, or in respect of an holyday, or of the new moon, or of the sabbath days: Which are a shadow of things to

come; but the body is of Christ.

Notice that this passage uses words that are similar to the previous texts such as holy day, and Sabbath days. Here these are referred to as "the shadow of things to come." The shadows were fulfilled and done away with by means of the death of our Lord Jesus. These feast days of the ceremonial system of laws that are referred to as the commandments written by Moses had no eternal connection as to the Sabbath of the Ten Commandments, which were personally written by God. Therefore, they have nothing in comparison to do with the seventh-day Sabbath, which has an eternal purpose.

Paul stated that the law is spiritual (Rom. 7:14). David declares that the law of God is perfect, converting the soul (Ps. 19:7). Ellen G. White wrote, "In the precepts of His holy law, God has given a perfect rule of life; and He has declared that until the close of time this law, unchanged in a single jot or tittle, is to maintain its claim upon human beings. Christ came to magnify the law and make it honorable.… In His own life He gave an example of obedience to the law of God" (*The Faith I Live By*, p. 86).

Psalm 111:7, 8 reads, "The works of his hands

are verity and judgment; all his commandments are sure. They stand fast for ever and ever, and are done in truth and uprightness." Therefore, there is no doubt that the Ten Commandments existed with God in the very beginning, mentioned in John 1:1, 2. Before anything was created or made, the Ten Commandment law—the everlasting law of God—was already in existence as the governing principle of God's heavenly kingdom. This law had to be established even before the angels and Lucifer were created. For it had to be in place already for it to be the standard of their obedience in God's kingdom at the time of their creation.

The law of God, perfect and eternal, came from the God who also is perfect and eternal. Biblical documentation makes it clear that for Lucifer and the fallen angels to be cited for committing sin, there had to be a law in place. That law had no condemnation upon them as long as they loved God with all their hearts, and served Him joyfully. But the law was used for their condemnation after they sinned, and refused to repent.

The last part of Romans 4:15 says, "For where no law is, there is no transgression." "But sin is not imputed when there is no law" (Rom. 5:13).

"Whosoever committed sin, transgresseth also the law, for sin is the transgression of the law" (1 John 3:4).

These passages attest to the fact that the law the Ten Commandments was already in existence before the angels were created. It is revealed that the heavenly government of God was already established before the creation of the angels. God's law was written on their hearts. Lucifer, the first sinner, led the angels in breaking the precept, "Thou shall have no other gods before me" (Exod. 20:3). To see some of the other Bible references with regard to Lucifer's sin, read also John 8:44 and 1 John 3:8.

Three Major Beginnings

There are three major beginnings recorded in the Bible: John 17:5 tells about the very first "beginning." Here Jesus spoke of having been with the father before the foundation of the world: "And now, O Father, glorify thou me with thine own self with the glory which I had with thee before the world was." In verse 24 it says: "Father, I will that they also, whom thou hast given me, be with me where I am; that they may behold my glory, which thou hast given me: for thou lovedst me before the foundation of the world." Again this first beginning is recorded in John 1:1, 2: "In the beginning was the Word, and the Word was with God, and the Word was God. The same was in the beginning with God."

The second reference to beginnings mentions Lucifer as a murderer from the beginning of his rebellion, which was before the creation of the earth. "He was a murderer from the beginning" (John 8:44).

The third beginning is found in Genesis 1:1: "In the beginning God created the heaven and earth." This is the beginning of our existence.

To review: Lucifer, at his creation, had the knowledge of the laws that govern the kingdom of God. This was in heaven long before Sinai, Israel, or even our creation. Jesus is the author of the law before the foundation of the world. Therefore, since the law was already established with the Godhead in heaven before any of their creative works, it follows that the seventh-day Sabbath was already formulated and originated in heaven, because it is seen written in the law by God.

Thus, at the creation of this world "the evening and morning" were omitted from the declaration of the seventh-day Sabbath because God wanted to initiate the infinite existence of the atmosphere of worship that existed in heaven before our time. The other six days of the weekly cycle of seven days, as we can see, was for the purpose of putting humanity in harmony with God's law of universal worship. In the embodiment of God's holy law it reveals that the fourth commandment regarding the seventh-day Sabbath was already in existence with God's law.

This is why the only day that was not started with evening and the morning was the seventh-day Sabbath, because of its spiritual and infinite nature as a part of the eternal law of God regarding worship. That day was placed at the completion of God's creative work as a memorial, not only of creation, but also of God's rest-day. It is the Sabbath, which God observed as His divine example for us. It is this text that has brought this wonderful inspiration to my mind when I notice that the words "evening and morning" were not use for the seventh day as it was for the completion of the previous six days. This thought, which the Spirit of God kept impressing on me, is what caused me to write this book about the divine clarity of the Sabbath.

> Thus the heavens and the earth were finished, and all the host of them. And on the seventh day God ended his work which he had made; and he rested on the seventh day from all his work which he had made. And God blessed the seventh day, and sanctified it: because that in it he had rested from all his work which God created and made. (Gen. 2:1–3)

So the seventh day was already instituted in the divine law of God called the Ten

Commandments long before there were Jews. At its dispensation to God's people, we are told that the law was the only portion of the Bible that was not entrusted to holy men of God, because I believe God wanted to convey its distinct divine nature Himself by writing the law with His own finger on two tablets of stone. This indeed shows the divine sovereignty of God's commandments and of the seventh day of rest that he made holy. As we examine the commandments, it is plain to see that this rest day the seventh-day Sabbath is placed in the midst of the whole law of God.

We can see a pattern here. When God placed the tree of the knowledge of good and evil in Eden to test the loyalty of His human children, He put it in the midst of the garden. He commanded them to eat of every tree of the garden, but not to eat of the tree of the knowledge of good and evil. So it is that when God instituted the Sabbath for human beings, He placed it in the midst of the law and commanded His people to remember it, hallow it, and reverence it. He told them to work on every other day of the week, but not to work on the Sabbath. He has placed the Sabbath also as a sign upon those whom He would sanctify through its observance.

He blessed the seventh day so that humanity

would receive the blessing inherent in it. Because it is part of God's holy law, the seventh-day Sabbath is likewise considered to be holy. Because God sanctified the Sabbath, people would become holy in keeping it, for it is designed to be forever holy in the presence of God. Jesus kept the seventh-day Sabbath holy when he was here on earth, so we can deduct that He kept the Sabbath not only at Creation, but also in heaven.

Luke 4:16 reads as follows: "And he came to Nazareth, where he had been brought up: and, as his custom was he went into the synagogue on the Sabbath day and stood up for to read." Matthew 5:17–19 reads: "Think not that I am come to destroy the law, or the prophets; I am not come to destroy, but to fulfill." Now let's look at John 14:15, 21: "If, ye love me, keep my Commandments.… He that hath my commandments, and keepeth them, he it is that loveth me: and he that loveth me shall be loved of my father, and I will love him and will manifest myself to him." John 15:10 reads: "If ye keep my commandments, ye shall abide in my love; even as I have kept my father's commandments, and abide in his love."

The experience of Adam's fall is a warning to us, so long as time last, that we are not to allow anyone to deceive us by man's theological words or the temptations of any angels that would detract one jot or tittle from the sacred formula of the law of Jehovah.

The weekly outpouring of the manna from heaven that fed the Israelites is another conclusive evidence that the Sabbath day is very sacred to God. Exodus 16:26–30 reads:

> Six days ye shall gather it; but on the seventh day, which is the sabbath, in it there shall be none. And it came to pass, that there went out some of the people on the seventh day for to gather, and they found none. And the Lord said unto Moses, How long refuse ye to keep my commandments and my laws? See, for that the Lord hath given you the sabbath, therefore he giveth you on the sixth day the bread of two days; abide ye every man in his place, let no man go out of his place on the seventh day. So the people rested on the seventh day.

Jesus said, "The Sabbath was made for man and not man for the Sabbath" (Mark 2:27).

In reality when Jesus speaks of man in general, it includes humanity in any creative form. In its divine composite, the Sabbath was made for human beings to distinguish their loyalty to their Maker and to His law. There is nothing we can do to add to or subtract from the Sabbath, for it is spiritually tailored to be a perfect fit for all humanity. We must follow the Creator's example and purpose for its design. We are not allowed to alter its purpose, because humans were not made for the Sabbath, but rather the Sabbath was made for humanity (Mark 2:27). As the earth became devastated by sin, the Sabbath is designed to help bring the minds of the people back towards their Creator. The Sabbath reiterates the fact that He is still our eternal God, Jehovah.

> If thou turn away thy foot from the sabbath, from doing thy pleasure on my holy day; and call the sabbath a delight, the holy of the Lord, honourable; and shalt honour him, not doing thine own ways, nor finding thine own pleasure, nor speaking thine own words: Then shalt thou delight thyself in the Lord; and I will cause thee to ride upon the high places of the earth,

and feed thee with the heritage of
Jacob thy father: for the mouth of the
Lord hath spoken it. (Isa. 58:13, 14)

God made the Sabbath for humanity, and
then gave us the instructions we need in order to
fulfill its purpose. He has told us how to keep it
holy. He did not leave it to people to formulate
ways to observe it, but by His own example He
has shown us how it must be kept.

Exodus 20:9 says, "Six days shalt thou labor
and do all thy work." God followed this rule when
He took six days to complete all of His creative
work. Exodus 20:10 says, "But the seventh day is
the Sabbath of the Lord thy God. In it thou shalt
not do any work." Genesis 2:1–3 states:

Thus the heavens and the earth were
finished, and all the host of them.
And on the seventh day God ended
his work which he had made; and he
rested on the seventh day from all his
work which he had made. And God
blessed the seventh day, and sanctified it: because that in it he had rested
from all his work which God created
and made.

So we can see that we are simply following God's example when we keep the seventh-day Sabbath as He did. He does not ask us to do anything that He has not done Himself. He bids us to follow His lead, for it will be of benefit to us. He has blessed that day and made it holy so that it may be a blessing to us.

Is the seventh-day Sabbath just another "shadow of things to come" that would eventually dissipate with time? Certainly not! Isaiah 66:23 reads, "And it shall come to pass that form one new moon to another and from one Sabbath to another shall all flesh come to worship before me, saith the Lord." The Sabbath day is a beautiful memorial of the creation, commemorating the birthday of this world. It also stands as a memorial of the deliverance from the bondage of sin. These memorials will continue even when we reside in the new heaven and earth throughout eternity.

> And the Lord spake unto Moses, saying, Speak thou also unto the children of Israel, saying, Verily my sabbaths ye shall keep: for it is a sign between me and you throughout your generations; that ye may know that I am the Lord

that doth sanctify you. Ye shall keep the sabbath therefore; for it is holy unto you: every one that defileth it shall surely be put to death: for whosoever doeth any work therein, that soul shall be cut off from among his people. Six days may work be done; but in the seventh is the sabbath of rest, holy to the Lord: whosoever doeth any work in the sabbath day, he shall surely be put to death. Wherefore the children of Israel shall keep the sabbath, to observe the sabbath throughout their generations, for a perpetual covenant. It is a sign between me and the children of Israel for ever: for in six days the Lord made heaven and earth, and on the seventh day he rested, and was refreshed. And he gave unto Moses, when he had made an end of communing with him upon mount Sinai, two tables of testimony, tables of stone, written with the finger of God. (Exod. 31:12–18)

The Sabbath day will also commemorate man's redemption throughout all eternity. Every

Sabbath, all the redeemed from this earth will gather together to celebrate the great victory wrought through Christ in the earth made new (see Isa. 66:22, 23).

Again we see that the origin of the Sabbath day is from eternity past, and it will continue the same throughout eternity in the future. With this in mind we can see why Paul says, "Do we then make void the law through faith? God forbid: yea, we establish the law" (Rom 3:31).

The Sabbath distinguishes between the true and false systems of worship that are in the world today. Romans 6:16 reads: "Know ye not, that to whom ye yield yourselves servants to obey, his servants ye are to whom ye obey; whether of sin unto death, or of obedience unto righteousness?"

Matthew 4:10 reads, "Thou shalt worship the Lord thy God and him only shalt thou serve." These last words, spoken by Jesus to Lucifer, indicate that we ought to be watchful for those who try to use feigned words against the truth. Like Jesus, we need to know the Scriptures for ourselves so we can discern between truth and error.

Matthew 15:9 says, "But in vain they do worship me, teaching for doctrines the commandments of men." It is this area that Jesus warned His disciples about when He told them to "take heed that no man deceive you. For many shall come in my name, saying, I am Christ; and shall deceive many" (Matt. 24:4, 5). Paul also warned, "Let no man deceive you by any means" (2 Thess. 2:3). Our safety and freedom in this regard is found in the following passage:

> But the Lord is faithful, who shall stablish you, and keep you from evil. And we have confidence in the Lord touching you, that ye both do and will do the things which we command you. And the Lord direct your hearts into the love of God, and into the patient waiting for Christ. (2 Thess. 3:3–5)

Remember, "we can do nothing against the truth, but for the truth" (2 Cor. 13:8).

"We ought to obey God rather than men" (Acts 5:29). "Choose you this day whom ye will serve" (Joshua 24:15).

The Sabbath was made as a sign by God, to identify His people. The Bible also indicates that it will be used as a spiritual mark or seal of Gods approval. This seal will be seen upon those who acknowledge the true form of worship, which was ordained by God through His holy law, the Ten

Commandments.

There are three essential markings on any official seal:

1. Name: Lord
2. Official position, title, or authority: Creator of everything
3. Extent of dominion: Heaven and earth

Only the fourth commandment contains the seal of the living God. This commandment alone of the Decalogue reveals all of the three dimensions of His seal: God's name, His authority, and His dominion. God alone is the Creator, the Sustainer, and even the Author and Finisher of our faith through our Lord and Savior Jesus Christ.

The Ten Commandments are listed in Exodus 20, and they read:

> And God spake all these words, saying, I am the Lord thy God, which have brought thee out of the land of Egypt, out of the house of bondage.
>
> Thou shalt have no other gods before me.
>
> Thou shalt not make unto thee any graven image, or any likeness of any thing that is in heaven above, or that is

in the earth beneath, or that is in the water under the earth: Thou shalt not bow down thyself to them, nor serve them: for I the Lord thy God am a jealous God, visiting the iniquity of the fathers upon the children unto the third and fourth generation of them that hate me; And shewing mercy unto thousands of them that love me, and keep my commandments.

Thou shalt not take the name of the Lord thy God in vain; for the Lord will not hold him guiltless that taketh his name in vain.

Remember the sabbath day, to keep it holy. Six days shalt thou labour, and do all thy work: But the seventh day is the sabbath of the Lord thy God: in it thou shalt not do any work, thou, nor thy son, nor thy daughter, thy manservant, nor thy maidservant, nor thy cattle, nor thy stranger that is within thy gates: For in six days the Lord made heaven and earth, the sea, and all that in them is, and rested the seventh day: wherefore the Lord blessed the sabbath day, and hallowed it.

Honour thy father and thy mother: that thy days may be long upon the land which the Lord thy God giveth thee.

Thou shalt not kill.

Thou shalt not commit adultery.

Thou shalt not steal.

Thou shalt not bear false witness against thy neighbour.

Thou shalt not covet thy neighbour's house, thou shalt not covet thy neighbour's wife, nor his manservant, nor his maidservant, nor his ox, nor his ass, nor any thing that is thy neighbour's.

And all the people saw the thunderings, and the lightnings, and the noise of the trumpet, and the mountain smoking: and when the people saw it, they removed, and stood afar off. And they said unto Moses, Speak thou with us, and we will hear: but let not God speak with us, lest we die. And Moses said unto the people, Fear not: for God is come to prove you, and that his fear may be before your faces, that ye sin not. (verses 1–20)

Let us also consider the following verses that speak to the importance of God's law and keeping the commandments:

> Let us hear the conclusion of the whole matter: Fear God, and keep his commandments: for this *is* the whole *duty* of man. For God shall bring every work into judgment, with every secret thing, whether *it be* good, or whether *it be* evil. (Eccles. 12:13, 14)

> And the dragon was wroth with the woman, and went to make war with the remnant of her seed, which keep the commandments of God, and have the testimony of Jesus Christ. (Rev. 12:17)

> Here is the patience of the saints: here *are* they that keep the commandments of God, and the faith of Jesus. (Rev. 14:12)

> To the law and to the testimony: if they speak not according to this word, *it is* because *there is* no light in them. (Isa. 8:20)

Blessed are they that do his commandments, that they may have right to the
tree of life, and may enter in through
the gates into the city. (Rev. 22:14)

Importance of the Sabbath

The remarkable discovery of the pre-existence of the Sabbath is one of many treasures of truth in the Word of God. The Bible was written by men who were under the inspiration of the Holy Spirit of God, and it is an infinite source of new insights. The Bible is indeed accurate. It is the authoritative Word of the living God.

In her book *The Great Controversy* Ellen White makes a statement about the ceaseless treasures of the eternal word of God and all that we will learn as we commune with the Creator: "Still there will arise new heights to surmount, new wonders to admire, new truths to comprehend, fresh objects to call forth the powers of the mind, soul, and body" (p. 677, 1911 edition).

Throughout eternity, our comprehension of the significance of the Sabbath will increase, but there will still be no divine change in the day, from the very first record of its institution at the creation of this world. It is a part of the law that expresses Jehovah's character, and God has said, "I change not" (Mal. 3 6).

The fact that the Ten Commandments were written by the finger of God, and not by human beings, reveals its divine authenticity. The law is holy unto God. The Sabbath commandment at the heart of the Ten Commandments has its origin with God, not only in heaven but here on earth. It was given when this earth was created, showing its sacredness when God kept it with our first parents. He taught Adam and Eve how to observed it, and commissioned them to teach its requirements to all of their descendants.

Adam was just about one day old when he kept the first Sabbath. The earth was six days old when the Sabbath was put in place. Everything that was made was sealed with the blessing, the sanctification, and the holiness of the seventh-day Sabbath, which completed the full cycle of the first week of creation. Even when Adam and Eve were removed from the Garden of Eden because of the fall, the seventh-day Sabbath remained as a divine institution to keep people in the habit of worshipping the true and living God, the Creator of all worlds throughout the universe.

The earth, symbolized by that one lost sheep (see Matt. 18:12–14), became a special project of interest for the Trinity of heaven. God committed the resources of the universe to His effort for the restoration of humanity. He plans to bring the earth back into the fold of the kingdom of God. In all of this, no change was made to the purpose of God in regard to the observance of the Sabbath. The impact of sin only made the holy day more important to our world. As the divine beacon of truth, the Sabbath is no doubt the means through which the worship of the true God, the Creator of heaven and earth, and the fountains of waters, is to be kept before the minds of all rational beings. This is divinely ordained according to the Bible.

Friend, remember the Sabbath day to keep it holy. God did not change, alter, or nail the Ten Commandments to the cross, as some indicate. Through this brief study we have established from the Bible the fact that the seventh-day Sabbath is of an eternal nature because of its placement within the eternal moral law of God.

Finally, in heaven and on earth conformity to the will of God is the only safe path. This is true not only for our time but throughout all eternity. Amen and amen!

We invite you to view the complete
selection of titles we publish at:

www.TEACHServices.com

Scan with your mobile
device to go directly
to our website.

Please write or email us your praises, reactions, or
thoughts about this or any other book we publish at:

TEACH Services, Inc.
P U B L I S H I N G
www.TEACHServices.com ● (800) 367-1844

P.O. Box 954
Ringgold, GA 30736

info@TEACHServices.com

TEACH Services, Inc., titles may be purchased in bulk for
educational, business, fund-raising, or sales promotional use.
For information, please e-mail:

BulkSales@TEACHServices.com

Finally, if you are interested in seeing
your own book in print, please contact us at

publishing@TEACHServices.com

We would be happy to review your manuscript for free.

www.ingramcontent.com/pod-product-compliance
Lightning Source LLC
LaVergne TN
LVHW021548080426
835509LV00019B/2911